Innocent Art

Innocent Art

Edited by David Larkin

with an Introduction and Biographical Notes by Martin Green
Picture Research by Celestine Dars

Ballantine Books   New York

Printed in Italy by Mondadori, Verona

We are most grateful to the artists, private collectors
and museums who have kindly allowed the use of material
in their copyright.

This edition published 1974
by Ballantine Books
201 East 50th Street, New York, N.Y. 10022

What is generally and collectively known as primitive art is more accurately described if we apply the words innocent or naive to it. In essence it is nonce art, it has no past and no future, it captures 'now' and freezes it forever. Whereas the trained, self-conscious artist cannot ignore the art of his predecessors, nor his contemporaries, the innocent or naive works as if he were the first man alive. He creates visual images of the world around him or the world of his imagination without a barrier of tradition. This is what gives naive paintings their immediacy, their delight and surprise. The philistine confronted by a late Picasso says, 'My child could do as good as that.' Confronted by true innocence, he is silenced. It is impossible to imitate innocence, and innocent art is not childish, it is childlike, uncorrupted.

Innocent or naive painters can, of course, be highly sophisticated artists, as they can equally be peasants or artisans. With Henri Rousseau it is difficult to know how much this McGonagall of painting was fooling or being fooled. Well known to the expressionist painters of his day, he was mocked behind his back by them, but fêted in public. His work hangs alongside theirs today.

But naive art must be distinguished from the *faux-naïf* art that can be seen hanging on the railings of Green Park and in Washington Square on Sunday mornings — 'airport art,' which the tourist buys on his way home. It is not only distinguished because it is painted without the thought of profit, but because it springs from a sense of joy or wonder at the visible world around us. It has the primeval excitement of existence.

It is also distinguished from amateur art or Sunday painting. The amateur artist, like Winston Churchill, tries to emulate the technique or mannerism of the artist proper. He doesn't copy nature, he copies technique, and he inevitably fails because it is impossible to copy genius. The innocent artist finds his own technique, his mind is not trammeled with advice, rules, strictures or conventions.

When the innocent eye paints what he sees, either in front of him or in his imagination, the image is transferred directly from his consciousness to the canvas, or whatever, without being filtered. The naive achieves his goal in a way that can take an artist who has undergone professional training years of study to achieve. The professional has to master a technique in order to free himself, the innocent is born free.

Innocent art has no message. It is a manifestation of joy which takes us back into the Garden of Eden into which we were all born and which has been stolen from us by knowledge.

PLATE 1

To William Uhde, the critic, who had retired from Paris to Senlis in 1912, **Séraphine Louis** *(born 1864 Arsy, died 1942 Clermont)* was just a charlady. That is, until he saw a still-life at a neighbor's house which he much admired. The painting was by his own cleaning woman, and he thereafter provided her with canvas and paint to unleash her fantastic imagination, as in her 'Garden of Eden' here.

PLATES 2, 3

These two paintings are by a typographer-turned-painter, **Dominique-Paul Peyronnet** *(born 1878 Telencen, near Bordeaux, died 1943)*. The exactitude demanded by his first profession is expressed in the sea, which has the fixed quality of a relief map, and in the rigid attention of his villagers as they listen to the announcement of the rural policeman.

PLATE 4

This portrait of the artist's wife is by the most famous of the primitive painters, **Henri Julien Félix Rousseau, 'Le Douanier'** *(born 1844 Laval, died 1910)*. The son of a tinsmith, Rousseau spent his military service in the regimental band – he was a talented musician – and married Clémence Boitard after completing it. He also served later in the Franco-Prussian war of 1870-71 and claimed that he saw action in Mexico. He finally became a customs officer in Paris, whence he acquired his appellation, and his art attracted many admirers. Between 1886 and 1910 he exhibited at the Salon des Indépendants. As was McGonagall, he was unmercifully mocked by his contemporaries and he survived with dignity a banquet given in his 'honor' by Picasso, at which were present Georges Braque, Marie Laurencin, Guillaume Apollinaire, Max Jacob, Gertrude Stein and many other artists.

PLATE 5

This picture of a young boy with his rabbit has many of the obsessions of the innocent painter, particularly the attention to the flowers in the background. It is painted by **Györy Stefula** *(born 1913)* who was born in Hamburg of a Hungarian father and French mother.

PLATE 6

Cats are typical subjects of innocent painters, as is this by **André Duranton** *(born 1905 Paris)*, who started his working life decorating silks and designing fabrics. The studios where he worked closed after the financial crash of 1929 when Duranton became a commercial traveller. Forced to work in a factory at the beginning of the last war, he later became a cinema projectionist. Afterwards, he took up his old trade of fabric design and began painting for his own pleasure.

PLATES 7, 8, 9, 10, 11, 12, 13, 14

There is a whole school of naive painters from Yugoslavia which has emerged since the last war. Many of them belong to what has been dubbed the 'school of Hlebine,' and most of them are of peasant origin. In most cases their biographies are similar, i.e. after finishing formal education they spent two years doing military service before taking jobs and finally becoming painters. Not untypical of this school is **Mijo Kovaćić** *(born 1935 Gorma Suma, near Hlebine)*, whose paintings here (7 & 8) depict peasant or country life in the grip of winter. He was taught painting-behind-glass by Ivan Generalić, the father of **Josip Generalić** *(born 1936)*, whose painting 'The Masks' (9) is again of a peasant winter scene. Generalić went to training college after completing his military service where he studied art and physical education. **Milan Rasic** *(born 1931)*, whose painting 'Springtime' (10) is reproduced here, is a Serbian peasant naive who took up painting in 1960. His work has been exhibited in Europe and Mexico and is full of insouciance and native gaiety. Of an older generation of peasant naives is **Ivan Rabuzin** *(born 1919 Croatia)*. A miner's son, he began to draw in 1944, and his landscapes (11 & 12) have a surreal quality, the flowers dwarfing the trees. Rabuzin was a cabinet maker but has painted professionally since 1962.

Another peasant naive in the same mold as the 'school of Hlebine' is **Ivan Lacković** *(born 1932 Batinska, Podravina)*, who began his artistic career copying local saints on the walls. After becoming known to the Gallery of Primitive Art in Zagreb, he moved and now works there for the Post Office. His paintings depict his rural background, as does 'Flood' (13) here,

and he says of his work, 'My pictures are like a debt that must be repaid to my true home.' Finally, in the same vein, there is **Macksimović Borivos,** whose work is typical of the whole of the peasant naive school. 'My Cow' (14) suggests perhaps that it is some time since the artist actually milked one, but the picture nevertheless transcends its sentimentality.

PLATE 15
In this anonymous American painting of a blacksmith's forge we have all the pride and dignity of the craftsman about his business. Everything is in its place, as Samuel Smiles would have it, the hammers, the tongs, and the jobs to be done. This is life before you would have unwittingly to trust your local garage to get your mass-produced mechanical transport back on the road. If the men in this picture shod your horse with a faulty shoe or put a crooked rim on your cart's wheel they would be more surprised than you would.

PLATE 16
This is a picture that records recent history. Airplanes are seen unloading bombs over a native village defended by soldiers armed only with rifles. It is in fact by an anonymous Ethiopian and the planes belonged to Mussolini's Italy. On the left, a white journalist (Evelyn Waugh, perhaps?) is smoking a cigarette and hammering what must be a typewriter; on the right is a small, bearded figure (surely Haile Selassie!) with a pith helmet and a machine-gun.

PLATE 17

This rich painting of a luxuriant garden is by **Maurice Grimaldi** *(born 1890 near Nancy, died 1968 Paris)*, who worked for the Post Office under another naive French painter, Louis Vivan. He took up painting after having served in the First World War, originally working with his son's own color-box.

PLATES 18, 19

Jules Lefranc *(born 1887 Laval)* comes from the birthplace of Henri Rousseau in France, though born some forty years later. His parents owned a hardware shop and he was first encouraged to paint by Claude Monet. He went into business on his own account in 1911 and he served in the army throughout the First World War. He later met the writer Louis Aragon and the painter René Rimbert, with whom he became friends in 1928 when he gave up business entirely in order to paint. His pictures are ungiving and exacting, particularly this view of the Eiffel Tower which has the eerie stillness of a city without people.

PLATE 20

A rare American naive painter is **Gertrude O'Brady** *(born 1901 Chicago)*. She left America for France, where she was interned for the duration of the war. Her picture here has the composed formality of an early photograph.

PLATE 21

A fair proportion of primitive or naive painters have been craftsmen by profession, as was **Alois Sauter** *(born 1875 Stabrook, Belgium, died 1952)*, who was a cabinet-maker. He lived later in Montreuil, near Paris, where he ran a workshop with his brother. The two brothers and the interior of the workshop, together with the artist's wife, are pictured here in proud detail.

PLATE 22

This 'Musician' is by an artist about whom little is known except what he reveals to his dealer at the Portal Gallery. **Fred Aris** is 'about forty,' keeps very much to himself and is apparently a café proprietor in south-east London. He is a slow and meticulous painter who is yet to have a full one-man show. His paintings of sailors and cats are hypnotic and haunting.

PLATE 23

This charming picture of the café by **F. Boilanges** captures the apparent complacency of the French bourgeoisie. Nevertheless, it is a complacency that enabled the French to produce Rimbaud, Verlaine and Baudelaire, apart from a nation that can passionately embrace modern technology.

PLATE 24

Primitive peoples have always made propitiatory offerings to various gods and there is a whole tradition of peasant votive painting in Europe and elsewhere. This is a typical example of a votive painting from Catania, in Sicily, in which is shown the disaster from which this peasant's family were saved by the saint's miraculous intercession.

PLATES 25, 26

Like the subject matter of many of his paintings, **Camille Bombois** *(born 1883 Venarey les Laumes, France)*, himself worked as a wrestler in circuses and fairgrounds. His childhood was spent on a barge and he later worked on a farm before going into the circus. He began to draw at sixteen and he was discovered by a journalist in 1922, when he exhibited his work on a Paris pavement in Montparnasse.

PLATE 27

This modern, innocent painting of a sporting winter scene has the flavor of those marvelous early Dutch snow-covered landscapes. Otherwise 'static' – even the figures seem frozen – snow is driving across from the left of **F. von Reiger's** picture, about to blot out the skaters entirely.

PLATE 28

In common with the naive painter Louis Vivan, **René Rimbert** *(born 1896 Paris)* worked for the Post Office as a clerk. A friend of Jules Lefranc, Max Jacob and Marcel Gromaire, Rimbert's paintings of the squares and streets of his native city liken him to a kind of naive Utrillo.

PLATE 29

Adolf Dietrich *(born 1877 Berlingen, Switzerland, died 1957)* was of peasant stock, as his patient and detailed pictures of animals suggest. As a child he worked with any material he could

before graduating to paint and brushes. He worked variously as a railwayman, rope-maker and woodcutter, before he was encouraged to devote himself solely to painting by the painter Völmy, from Basel. In 1916 his drawings were published in the *Book of Lake Constance* and he worked almost exclusively as a painter from 1926 until his death. His lakeside painting reproduced here – with all the ripe grapes in the foreground – does not suggest Switzerland at all to the Northern eye.

PLATE 30

All that is known about **Jean-Baptiste Guiraud** *(born 1892 at Saint Chignian-Apt de Saint Pont, Herault, France)* is what he himself tells us at the foot of his works, i.e. his name, place and date of birth. His subject matter is divided mainly between storm-tossed ships and Oriental India, as in the 'Chasse au tigre.' These Indian pictures look as though they may have been copied from a book of miniatures. Two portraits, of a man and of a woman, have survived, and the Berri-Lardy Gallery in Paris has spent the last twenty years fruitlessly seeking further biographical information.

PLATE 31

When **Arthur William Chesher** *(born 1897 Wootton, near Bedford, died 1973 within miles of Wootton)* was very young, he learned to drive a traction engine, and agricultural machinery became a life-long passion. He worked as a traction-engine driver until the 1940s, when two accidents forced him to give up his work.

The first was the loss of an eye as a result of a shot-gun wound, the second when he caught his arm in a threshing machine and it was left virtually useless. He started to paint agricultural machines, in exact detail and in their correct settings, and his work flowered into a pictorial history of steam agriculture in Britain from the mid-nineteenth century. His 'Bean Threshing Machine' is typical.

PLATE 32

Joseph Whiting Stock *(born 1815 Springfield, Massachusetts, died 1855)* was a naive American painter whose diary records over 900 portraits; this one, of a baby, was painted between the years 1842 and 1845. Crippled by an accident at the age of eleven he took up painting at seventeen. He worked mostly in his native Springfield, though he traveled as far as New Bedford, New Haven, Warren, Bristol and Providence, Rhode Island. Apart from portraits, he also painted miniatures, landscapes and occasionally marine subjects. His work is collected in the Museum of Modern Art, New York, and the Rockefeller Folk Art Collection.

PLATE 33

This picture, 'The Lehigh Canal,' is by another naive American painter, **Joseph Pickett** *(born 1848 New Hope, Pennsylvania, died 1918)*. He traveled with a circus, worked as a carpenter at local fairs, and ended up with his own shooting gallery in New Hope, for which he painted the background. He later owned a grocery shop, in the store-room of which he used to paint. He made up his own paints and brushes and sometimes spent months or years on a picture, but very few of them have survived.

PLATES 34, 35

The only British naive to have a painting in the Tate while he was still alive was **James Lloyd** *(born 1906 Alsager, Cheshire, died 1974 Spirkenbeck, Yorkshire)*, who first took up painting because of his interest in farm animals. He worked variously as a village policeman, lamplighter and on a farm. He served in the army in Europe in the Second World War and began to paint after his return to civilian life. His method of painting evolved not because he had any knowledge of 'Pointillism,' but because he copied subjects out of the *Farmer and Stockbreeder*, imitating the dots that make up photographic reproduction. He consequently used fine brushes and worked in gouache on whatever material came readily to hand. In 1953 his wife read an article about untrained painters and sent some of his work to Sir Herbert Read. Read was intrigued and went to visit Lloyd, accompanied by an art critic. Immediately convinced of the work's value they arranged an exhibition through the Arthur Jeffress Gallery. When this closed, Lloyd was taken up and encouraged by the Portal Gallery. Ken Russell chose him to play the role of Le Douanier himself when he made his film about Henri Rousseau, finding him perfect for the part. His paintings here show the incredible care with which they were built up, dot by dot.

PLATE 36

This celebration of the Liberation is by a French gardener-cum-primitive painter, **Auguste-André Bauchant** *(born 1873 Château Renault, died 1958)*, who painted mythological subjects, landscapes and flowers. He served in the First World War as a surveyor and cartographer. He was taken up by Le Corbusier, Ozenfant and Lipschitz, and Diaghilev commissioned him to do the stage decorations for Stravinsky's *Apollon Musagète.*

PLATE 37

A diamond-cutter by profession, **Salomon Meijers** *(born 1877 Amsterdam, died 1965 Laren)* began painting in 1914. He lived in Blaricum and his paintings of city scenes, animals – as in his 'Surprise Contents' – and still-lifes have that undeviating attention to detail that could be expected from a diamond-cutter.

PLATE 38

This somber painting of John Brown going to his hanging is by **Horace Pippin** *(born 1888 West Chester, Pennsylvania, died 1947)*, an eminent black naive painter. He began to paint religious scenes at the age of ten and sustained himself as a porter, foundry worker and antique dealer. He fought as a soldier in France in the First World War and painted his first work in oils in 1930. Apart from scenes from American Negro life, he painted landscapes, still-lifes and war pictures from memory.

PLATE 39

This fat family portrait was painted by the South American **F. Botero** *(born 1932 Medellin, Colombia)* who began his artistic career designing sets for the theater. He moved to Bogotà in 1951, before going to Spain, where he copied old masters in the Prado, and then to France and Italy. He returned to Bogotà in 1955, thereafter going to Mexico and Washington and finally ending up in New York. His admiration for the Mexican painter Diego Rivera is expressed in 'La Familia Pinzon.'

PLATE 40

It is difficult to associate this innocent nude with the background of this odd, Polish-American naive painter, **Morris Hirschfield** *(born 1872 Poland, died 1946 United States)*. As a child he carved figures for the church of his native town. He emigrated to the United States in 1890, where he went into the rag-trade. After working for a number of years he opened his own factory. He retired after a serious illness in 1936, when he began to paint.

1) l'Arbre de paradis
SERAPHINE LOUIS
1929
Musée d'Art Moderne, Paris

from
2) la Mer (the painter's last work)
DOMINIQUE PEYRONNET
1943
Private collection, Paris

3) l'Annonce du garde-champêtre
DOMINIQUE PEYRONNET
1940
Musée d'Art Moderne, Paris

4) la Femme de l'artiste dans un jardin
HENRI ROUSSEAU, called le Douanier Rousseau
Musée du Jeu de Paume, Paris

5) Young boy with rabbit
GYORY STEFULA
1957
Private collection, Munich

6) Cat
ANDRÉ DURANTON
1973
Galerie Berri Lardy, Paris

7) Bird of prey
MIJO KOVACIC
1962
Zagreb Gallery

8) Winter scene
MIJO KOVACIC
1968
Museum of Modern Art, Zagreb

from
9) The Masks
JOSIP GENERALIC
1968
Zagreb Gallery

10) Springtime
MILAN RASIC
Zagreb Gallery

11) Landscape
IVAN RABUZIN
1960
Collection Ledic, Zagreb

12) Landscape
IVAN RABUZIN
1966
Galerie Berri Lardy, Paris

13) Flood
IVAN LACKOVIC
Collection Ledic, Zagreb

14) My Cow
MACKSIMOVIC BORIVOS
Collection Ledic, Zagreb

15) Blacksmith shop

Unknown American Artist

Gift of Edgar William and Bernice Chrysler Garbisch
National Gallery of Art, Washington

16) Italian bombing of Ethiopia
Unknown Artist
1939
Collection Eric Lister, London

17) le Gros arbre
MAURICE GRIMALDI (GRIM)
Collection Holzinger, Munich

18) le Métro aérien
JULES LEFRANC
Musée d'Art Moderne, Paris

19) Flowers
JULES LEFRANC
1945
Galerie Berri Lardy, Paris

20) Promenade en barque
GERTRUDE O'BRADY
Collection J. Masurel, Paris

from
21) The cabinet-maker's workshop
ALOIS SAUTER
1931
Collection Felix Labisse, Paris

22) The Musician
FRED ARIS
1972
Portal Gallery, London

23) The Bistroquet
F. BOILANGES
Collection Jan Balet

MIRACOLO CONCESSO A CIANCIO MARIA, ARCIFA PAOLINA E ANTONINO DA BELPASSO. IL GIORNO 30-5-951

24) Ex-voto from Catania, Sicily
1951
Bayerisches Nationalmuseum, Munich

25) l'Athlète forain
CAMILLE BOMBOIS
c. 1930
Musée d'Art Moderne, Paris

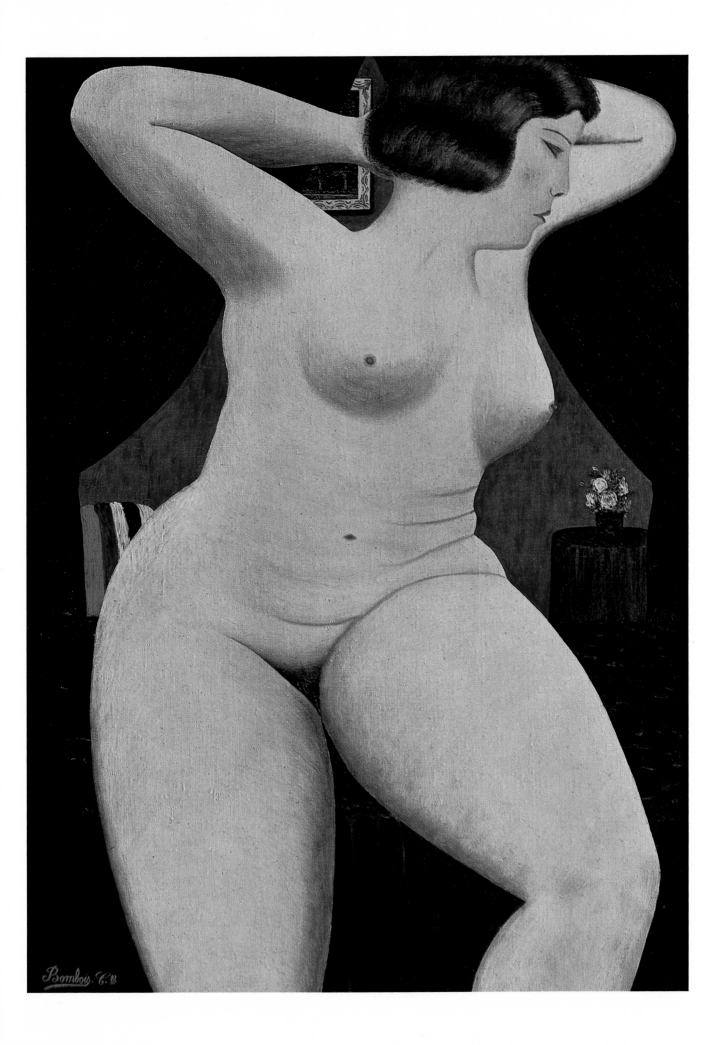

26) Nu aux bras levés
CAMILLE BOMBOIS
1925
Musée d'Art Moderne, Paris

27) Ice skating in Franconia
F. VON RIEGER
1967
Private collection, Italy

29) Paysage près de Steckborn
ADOLF DIETRICH
1945
Private collection, Bern

30) Chasse au tigre
JEAN-BAPTISTE GUIRAUD
1892
Galerie Berri Lardy, Paris

31) Bean threshing machine
ARTHUR W. CHESHER
1971
Portal Gallery, London

32) Portrait of a baby
JOSEPH WHITING STOCK
1840
Private collection, U.S.A.

33) Lehigh Canal, New York
JOSEPH PICKETT
Private collection, Switzerland

34) Watching the chickens
JAMES LLOYD
1972
Portal Gallery, London

35) The Kiss
JAMES LLOYD
1972
Portal Gallery, London

from
36) Fête de la Libération
AUGUSTE-ANDRE BAUCHANT
1945
Musée d'Art Moderne, Paris

37) Surprise contents
SALOMON MEIJERS
1909
Stedelijk Museum, Amsterdam

38) John Brown going to his hanging
HORACE PIPPIN
Pennsylvania Academy of Fine Arts, U.S.A.

39) la Familia Pinzon
F. BOTERO
Museum of Art, Rhode Island School of Design, U.S.A.

40) Girl in a mirror
MORRIS HIRSHFIELD
1940
Museum of Modern Art, New York